52-WEEK

DEVOTIONAL

FOR MOMS

Published by Midsummer Bloom Books

First Edition: September 2025
Printed in the United States of America

Contents

Introduction

Hi there. This book is for you—the real you. The one who sneaks away for five minutes of quiet in the bathroom, who's served cereal for dinner more than once, and who loves her children with every fiber of her being while quietly wondering if she's getting any of this right. You're not alone. This space is here to remind you of that.

Motherhood is beautiful, messy, exhausting, and sacred all at once. It's a calling that stretches us beyond what we thought possible and reveals both our deepest weaknesses and God's greatest strengths. Through sleepless nights and endless laundry, through first steps and teenage struggles, God is present in every moment—speaking truth and life into your weary soul.

This devotional isn't about adding more to your already full plate. It's about finding God right where you are—in the carpool line, during naptime, or in those precious quiet moments before the house wakes up. Each week offers a gentle rhythm: a truth from God's Word, a thought to ponder, a prayer to lift you up, a challenge to encourage growth, and a moment to pause and breathe.

You don't need to be a perfect mom. You just need to be a loved daughter of the King, doing your best with His help. Let these pages remind you—week after week—that you're not alone, you're deeply loved, and you're exactly the mom God chose for your children.

Week 1: You Are More Than "Mom"

God's Truth

"For we are his workmanship, created in Christ Jesus for good works, which God prepared beforehand, that we should walk in them."-Ephesians 2:10 (ESV)

Devotional Thought

Before little voices started calling you "Mom," God knew your name. He crafted you with intentional purpose, weaving together your personality, gifts, and dreams. Yes, motherhood is a beautiful part of your story, but it's not your whole story.

Sometimes we lose ourselves in the constant demands of mothering. We forget the woman who once had hobbies, dreams, and conversations that didn't revolve around naptime schedules. But God sees all of you—the mother, the woman, the unique creation He designed with specific purposes in mind.

You are His workmanship, His masterpiece. The Greek word for workmanship is "poiema," from which we get the word "poem." You are God's poem, His work of art. Every line of your life, including motherhood, contributes to the beautiful story He's writing.

Your identity isn't swallowed up by motherhood; it's enhanced by it. The gifts God placed in you didn't disappear when you became a mom—they found new expressions. Your creativity might now plan birthday parties. Your leadership might guide little hearts. Your compassion multiplies as you kiss scraped knees.

Remember today that while being "Mom" is a precious calling, you remain God's beloved daughter first. In His eyes, you are complete, valued, and purposeful beyond any single role you fill.

A Prayer for You

Father, remind me today that I am fearfully and wonderfully made. Help me embrace both my calling as a mother and my identity as Your beloved daughter. When I feel lost in the demands of motherhood, whisper my name and remind me of the unique woman You created me to be. Amen.

Your Challenge

This week, spend fifteen minutes doing something that reminds you of who you were before becoming a mom. Read a few pages of that book, listen to your favorite music, paint your nails, or call an old friend. Reconnect with a piece of yourself that brings you joy beyond your role as mother.

Take a Moment

Close your eyes and take three deep breaths. With each exhale, release one worry about your mothering. With each inhale, receive God's reminder that you are His beloved daughter, created with purpose and loved beyond measure.

Week 2: God's Strength for Weak Moments

God's Truth

"But he said to me, 'My grace is sufficient for you, for my power is made perfect in weakness.' Therefore I will boast all the more gladly of my weaknesses, so that the power of Christ may rest upon me."–2 Corinthians 12:9 (ESV)

Devotional Thought

Four in the morning. The baby's crying again. You stumble through the darkness, exhaustion weighing heavy on your shoulders. These are the moments when you feel most inadequate, when your weakness is impossible to hide. But here's the beautiful truth: God's power shines brightest in these exact moments.

We often believe we need to be strong for our children, to have it all together. We paste on smiles when we're crumbling inside, afraid that admitting weakness means we're failing. But God's economy works differently. He doesn't demand our strength; He offers His own.

When you snap at your toddler after the fifth meltdown of the day, grace is there. When you burn dinner while helping with homework, grace is there. When you cry in the shower because you feel like you're failing everyone, grace meets you there too.

Your weaknesses aren't obstacles to God's work in your life—they're opportunities. Every moment you feel inadequate is an invitation to lean into His sufficient grace. He doesn't expect you to mother in your own strength. He knows you can't, and that's exactly the point.

Today, instead of hiding your weakness, bring it to God. Let Him transform your not-enough into His more-than-enough.

A Prayer for You

Lord, I'm tired and weak today. Thank You that Your grace is sufficient for me. When I have nothing left to give, fill me with Your strength. Help me remember that my weaknesses are not failures but opportunities for Your power to shine through me. Amen.

Your Challenge

Today, when you hit a moment of weakness—losing patience, feeling exhausted, or making a mistake—pause and literally say out loud: "God's grace is sufficient for me." Let this truth sink into your bones. Watch how acknowledging your need for Him changes everything.

Take a Moment

Place your hand over your heart and feel it beating. That steady rhythm is God sustaining you, moment by moment. You don't have to be strong. You just have to be held.

Week 3: Breaking Free from Comparison

God's Truth

"Not that we dare to classify or compare ourselves with some of those who are commending themselves. But when they measure themselves by one another and compare themselves with one another, they are without understanding."–2 Corinthians 10:12 (ESV)

Devotional Thought

She makes organic lunches shaped like zoo animals. Her house looks like a magazine spread. Her children wear coordinating outfits without stains. Meanwhile, you're celebrating because everyone has on matching socks today. The comparison trap is real, and it's stealing your joy.

Social media has turned motherhood into a highlight reel where everyone else seems to be winning while you're barely surviving. But here's what those perfect posts don't show: every mom struggles. Every mom doubts. Every mom has days when dry cereal counts as breakfast and screen time saves sanity.

God didn't create you to be her—that other mom you're comparing yourself to. He created you to be exactly the mom your children need. Your style, your strengths, even your struggles are part of His perfect plan for your family.

Comparison blinds us to our own victories. While you're envying another mom's crafting skills, she might be wishing she had your patience. While you admire someone's organized home, she might long for your ability to laugh at chaos.

The truth is, there's no competition in God's kingdom. We're all on the same team, fighting the same battles, needing the same grace. Your motherhood journey is uniquely yours, crafted by a God who makes no mistakes.

A Prayer for You

Father, free me from the trap of comparison. Help me see my motherhood through Your eyes, not through filtered social media posts. Remind me that You chose me specifically for my children, and equip me to celebrate both my victories and others' without comparison. Amen.

Your Challenge

This week, every time you catch yourself comparing, stop and name one thing you're doing well as a mom. Build a mental list of your wins, no matter how small. Let gratitude for your unique journey replace the poison of comparison.

Take a Moment

Look at your hands. These hands that wipe tears, prepare meals, and give hugs are unlike any other mother's hands. They are specifically designed to love your children in ways no one else can.

Week 4: When You Feel Invisible

God's Truth

"She is clothed with strength and dignity; she can laugh at the days to come."–Proverbs 31:25 (ESV)

Devotional Thought

Another day of endless tasks that no one notices. Laundry folded, dishes washed, boo-boos kissed, stories read. You pour yourself out in a thousand small ways, yet it feels like no one sees. You wonder if what you're doing even matters when there's no applause, no recognition, just another day of the same invisible work.

But God sees every act of love. Every sandwich made, every nightmare soothed, every patient response to "Mom, watch this!" He sees the strength it takes to show up day after day for people who won't fully appreciate your sacrifice until they're adults.

Your work isn't invisible to the One who matters most. He's taking note of every selfless moment, every choosing of their needs over yours, every prayer whispered over sleeping children. These seemingly small acts are building something eternal—hearts shaped by consistent love.

The world might not celebrate the mom who remembers everyone's favorite snacks or who knows just how to calm each child's specific fears. But heaven celebrates you. Your

faithfulness in the unseen moments is preparing your children for their own callings.

You are clothed with strength and dignity, even in yoga pants and yesterday's ponytail. Your work matters immensely, even when no one says thank you.

A Prayer for You

Lord, when I feel invisible and unappreciated, remind me that You see everything. Help me find purpose in the hidden moments of motherhood. Strengthen me to continue serving with joy, knowing that my work is building Your kingdom in little hearts. Amen.

Your Challenge

This week, celebrate one "invisible" task you do each day. As you fold laundry, thank God for the people who wear these clothes. As you prepare meals, pray blessings over those who will eat them. Transform invisible work into visible worship.

Take a Moment

Stand tall and take a power pose—hands on hips, chin up. You are a warrior, fighting battles no one sees. Feel the strength God has placed within you.

Week 5: Finding Rest in Your Busy Days

God's Truth

"Come to me, all who labor and are heavy laden, and I will give you rest."–Matthew 11:28 (ESV)

Devotional Thought

Rest feels like a luxury you can't afford. There's always one more load of laundry, one more email to answer, one more mess to clean. You fall into bed exhausted only to wake up and do it all again. Jesus understands this weariness, and He's extending an invitation specifically to you.

Rest isn't just about sleep, though you probably need more of that too. It's about finding moments of peace in the chaos, little pockets of restoration throughout your day. Jesus doesn't say, "Come to me when you finally have time." He says come now, in your weariness, with your to-do list still full.

Sometimes rest looks like five minutes on the porch with your coffee while kids watch cartoons. Sometimes it's choosing to leave dishes in the sink and read that bedtime story extra slowly. Sometimes it's simply breathing deeply and remembering you're held by a God who never sleeps.

You don't have to earn rest. You don't have to finish everything first. Jesus offers rest in the middle of your labor, not after it's complete. He knows that motherhood doesn't offer many finish lines, so He meets you in the marathon.

Today, accept His invitation. Let Him carry what feels too heavy.

A Prayer for You

Jesus, I'm so tired. Help me find rest in You even when I can't stop moving. Teach me to recognize moments of grace throughout my day. Show me how to receive Your rest without guilt, knowing that You are holding all things together. Amen.

Your Challenge

Set a timer for three times today. When it goes off, stop whatever you're doing and take five deep breaths while repeating: "Jesus gives me rest." Let these mini-breaks reset your spirit throughout the day. Notice how these brief pauses change your perspective.

Take a Moment

Put your feet up right now, even if just for thirty seconds. Feel the weight leaving your legs. This is what Jesus wants to do for your soul—lift the weight, even briefly.

Week 6: Joy Amid Everyday Challenges

God's Truth

"The joy of the Lord is your strength."–Nehemiah 8:10b (ESV)

Devotional Thought

Joy feels elusive when you're cleaning up the third spilled cup of milk before 9 AM. When tantrums echo through grocery stores and homework battles rage at the kitchen table, joy seems like something for mothers with easier children or more patience. But God's joy isn't dependent on circumstances.

The joy of the Lord isn't the fleeting happiness of a smooth morning routine or a child's good behavior. It's deeper, steadier—a wellspring that bubbles up even in frustrating moments. This joy comes from knowing you're loved, knowing you're not alone, knowing this chaos has purpose.

Some days joy looks like dancing in the kitchen while making dinner, even though you're exhausted. Sometimes it's finding humor when your toddler decorates the wall with markers. Sometimes it's the quiet joy of watching your children sleep, finally peaceful after a day of battles.

Joy doesn't mean you're happy about every situation. It means you trust the God who's in control of them all. It means choosing to see gifts amid challenges: the strong will that frustrates you now will serve your child well later; the endless questions

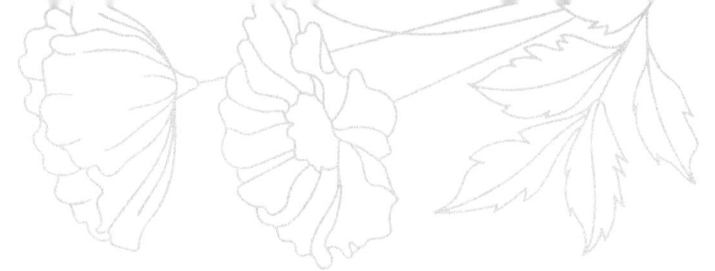

reveal a curious mind; the chaos means your home is full of life.

Today, dig deep for that joy. It's there, placed by God Himself, ready to be your strength.

A Prayer for You

Lord, when challenges steal my joy, remind me that true joy comes from You. Help me find reasons to smile today, even in difficulties. Fill me with Your joy that doesn't depend on perfect circumstances but on Your perfect love. Amen.

Your Challenge

Create a "joy jar" this week. Each day, write down one moment that brought you joy—your child's laugh, a unexpected hug, a successful bedtime. When challenges arise, remember these joy deposits. Let them remind you that difficulties don't erase beautiful moments.

Take a Moment

Smile right now, even if you don't feel like it. Hold it for ten seconds. Notice how your body responds to this simple act. Joy sometimes starts with choosing the posture before feeling the emotion.

Week 7: Gratitude That Changes Everything

God's Truth

"Give thanks in all circumstances; for this is the will of God in Christ Jesus for you."–1 Thessalonians 5:18 (ESV)

Devotional Thought

Gratitude in all circumstances—even when the washing machine breaks, the baby won't sleep, and your teenager won't talk? It seems impossible, even unreasonable. But God isn't asking you to be thankful for difficult circumstances; He's inviting you to find gratitude within them.

Gratitude is like putting on glasses that help you see clearly. Without them, all you notice are messes and frustrations. With them, you see blessings hidden in plain sight: children healthy enough to make messes, a home that needs cleaning because people live here, noise that means your house is full of life.

When you practice gratitude, something shifts. The same situation that felt overwhelming becomes manageable. Not because anything external changed, but because gratitude changes you. It softens hard edges, lifts heavy spirits, and opens your eyes to God's presence in ordinary moments.

Today's chaos is tomorrow's cherished memory. One day you'll miss these toys scattered everywhere, these constant requests for snacks, these bedtime negotiations. Gratitude helps you see the gift inside the struggle right now, not just in hindsight.

Start small. Thank God for one thing, even if it's just that this day will eventually end. Watch how that tiny seed of gratitude grows into something that changes everything.

A Prayer for You

Father, help me develop eyes that see reasons for gratitude everywhere. When I'm tempted to complain, prompt me to give thanks instead. Transform my perspective from what's lacking to what's abundant. Teach me that gratitude is my pathway to peace. Amen.

Your Challenge

Before your feet hit the floor each morning this week, name three things you're grateful for. Start your day with gratitude and watch how it colors everything that follows. Make this your new morning rhythm, setting the tone before chaos begins.

Take a Moment

Look around your space right now. Find five things that represent God's provision—a photo, a toy, a piece of furniture. Let your eyes rest on each one and whisper "thank you."

Week 8: Finding Laughter in Hard Moments

God's Truth

"A joyful heart is good medicine, but a crushed spirit dries up the bones."–Proverbs 17:22 (ESV)

Devotional Thought

When your toddler announces to the grocery store that "Mommy has hair on her bottom," you have two choices: mortification or laughter. When you discover your child fed the dog your anniversary dinner, you can cry or find the humor. Laughter truly is medicine, especially for weary mama hearts.

Some days feel heavy with responsibility, discipline, and endless needs. But God created laughter as a release valve, a way to let pressure escape before you explode. He knew motherhood would require this special kind of medicine—the ability to find humor when everything goes wrong.

Laughter doesn't minimize real struggles or mean you're not taking motherhood seriously. It means you're choosing not to let difficulties have the final word. When you laugh at the chaos instead of crying over it, you're declaring that joy is stronger than frustration.

Your children need to see you laugh. They need to know that mistakes aren't catastrophes, that imperfection can be funny, that joy exists even in difficult seasons. Your laughter teaches them resilience and shows them that life doesn't have to be perfect to be beautiful.

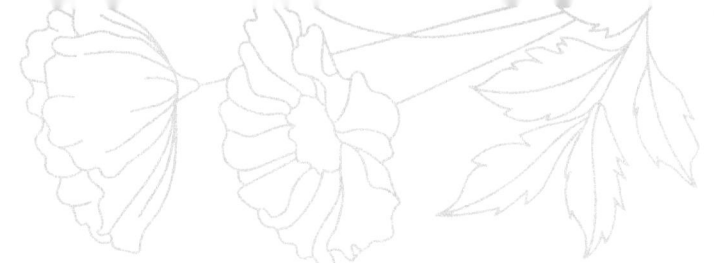

Today, look for reasons to laugh. Let yourself find humor in the absurdity of motherhood. Let laughter be your medicine.

A Prayer for You

Lord, help me find laughter even in frustrating moments. When I want to cry or yell, remind me to look for the humor. Give me a heart that chooses joy and laughter as medicine for my weary soul. Let my home ring with holy laughter. Amen.

Your Challenge

This week, when something goes wrong, ask yourself: "Will this be funny in five years?" If yes, choose to laugh now. Share the funny story with a friend. Let laughter lighten your load and remind you that perfection isn't the goal—joy is.

Take a Moment

Think of the funniest thing your child has said or done recently. Let yourself laugh out loud about it right now. Feel how laughter literally lightens your body.

Week 9: Celebrate the Small Wins

God's Truth

"Let us not become weary in doing good, for at the proper time we will reap a harvest if we do not give up."–Galatians 6:9 (ESV)

Devotional Thought

Everyone brushed their teeth without a reminder. Your picky eater tried one bite of vegetables. You made it through Target without a meltdown. These might seem like tiny victories, but in the marathon of motherhood, small wins matter immensely.

We're often so focused on big goals—raising kind humans, building strong faith, creating lasting memories—that we miss the small victories happening daily. But God sees every small faithful step. He celebrates with you when your child shares without prompting or when you respond patiently to the tenth "why" question.

These small wins are building blocks of the harvest Paul mentions. Each one matters. Every patient response is teaching emotional regulation. Every bedtime prayer is planting faith seeds. Every "please" and "thank you" enforced is building character.

Motherhood rarely offers dramatic victories. Instead, it's a collection of small wins that add up to transformed lives. Your child won't suddenly become responsible; they'll slowly learn through a thousand small moments of follow-through. They won't instantly develop faith; it'll grow through countless bedtime prayers and everyday conversations about God.

Today, notice and celebrate small wins. They're evidence that your faithful work is producing fruit, even when progress feels invisible.

A Prayer for You

Father, help me recognize and celebrate small victories in my mothering. When I feel like I'm not making progress, remind me that You see every faithful act. Give me eyes to notice the tiny wins that are building Your kingdom in my children's hearts. Amen.

Your Challenge

Keep a "wins list" this week on your phone or a sticky note. Record every small victory, no matter how tiny. Your child said sorry without prompting? Write it down. Everyone ate dinner together? That counts. Review your list when you feel discouraged.

Take a Moment

Hold your hands out, palms up. Imagine each small win from today dropping into your hands like golden coins. Feel their weight. These are treasures you're collecting for eternity.

Week 10: The Power of Saying "Yes"

God's Truth

"Let what you say be simply 'Yes' or 'No'; anything more than this comes from evil."–Matthew 5:37 (ESV)

Devotional Thought

"Mom, can we make cookies?" "Will you play with me?" "Can we have a dance party?" Your day is filled with requests, and your default might be "no" because yes means mess, time, or energy you don't have. But sometimes, strategic yeses create the memories that matter most.

Not every yes needs to be elaborate. Yes to reading one more story. Yes to letting them help with dinner, even though it'll take longer. Yes to staying up five minutes past bedtime for extra snuggles. These simple yeses tell your children they matter more than schedules or clean kitchens.

Of course, you can't say yes to everything. Boundaries matter, and no is sometimes the most loving answer. But consider what drives your answers. Are you saying no from exhaustion, or because the request genuinely isn't good? Are you missing connection opportunities because yes feels inconvenient?

Some of your best motherhood memories will come from unexpected yeses. The spontaneous puddle jumping. The impromptu living room campout. The random Tuesday ice cream for dinner. These yeses break routine and create magic.

Today, look for one opportunity to say yes when you'd normally say no. Watch your child's face light up. That joy is worth whatever inconvenience follows.

A Prayer for You

Lord, give me wisdom to know when to say yes and when to say no. Help me see past inconvenience to opportunity. Show me how to create joy through strategic yeses while maintaining healthy boundaries. Let my yeses build connection with my children. Amen.

Your Challenge

This week, say yes to one request each day that you'd typically refuse—if it's safe and reasonable. Notice how these yeses affect your family's atmosphere. Document the memories created by stepping outside your comfort zone into connection.

Take a Moment

Nod your head yes right now, several times. Feel how this physical movement of agreement opens something in your spirit. Carry this openness into your next interaction with your children.

Week 11: Creating Calm in the Crazy

God's Truth

"And he said to them, 'Come away by yourselves to a desolate place and rest a while.' For many were coming and going, and they had no leisure even to eat."–Mark 6:31 (ESV)

Devotional Thought

Your home sounds like a zoo, looks like a tornado hit, and feels like Grand Central Station. Everyone needs something right now, voices are rising, and you're about to lose it. In these moments, you have the power to shift the atmosphere from chaos to calm.

Jesus understood the need to create calm spaces amid busy life. Even He withdrew from crowds to find peace. You might not be able to escape to a desolate place, but you can create pockets of calm within your chaos.

Sometimes creating calm means lowering your voice when you want to yell. Your quiet tone can de-escalate rising tensions faster than any stern words. Sometimes it means putting on soft music, lighting a candle, or declaring a five-minute "quiet time" where everyone finds a cozy spot.

You set the emotional temperature of your home. When you remain calm, it ripples outward. This doesn't mean suppressing frustration or pretending everything's fine. It means choosing to be the eye of the storm, the steady presence your children can count on.

Creating calm is a practice, not perfection. Some days you'll fail spectacularly. But each time you choose calm over chaos, you're teaching your children emotional regulation and showing them that peace is possible even in difficult moments.

A Prayer for You

Father, when chaos surrounds me, help me be an anchor of calm. Give me supernatural peace that passes understanding. Help me create an atmosphere where my children feel safe and settled, even when life feels overwhelming. Be my peace in every storm. Amen.

Your Challenge

This week, when chaos erupts, try the "whisper method." Instead of raising your voice, lower it to almost a whisper. Watch how your children lean in to hear you and how the atmosphere shifts. Use your calm as a superpower to transform your home's energy.

Take a Moment

Place one hand on your chest and one on your belly. Breathe slowly, feeling your belly expand. This is your calm-creating breath. Practice it now so you can access it in chaos.

Week 12: Praying Bold Prayers for Your Kids

God's Truth

"The prayer of a righteous person has great power as it is working."–James 5:16b (ESV)

Devotional Thought

Your prayers for your children carry power you can't fully comprehend. Every whispered prayer over a sleeping baby, every desperate plea during teenage years, every grateful acknowledgment of growth—these prayers are working in ways you may not see for years.

Don't underestimate your prayers because they feel simple or repetitive. God isn't looking for eloquence; He's looking for faith. Your "Help!" prayers matter as much as lengthy intercessions. Your consistent covering of your children in prayer is building a foundation that will hold them through every season.

Pray bold prayers. Ask God to use your children mightily for His kingdom. Pray for their future spouses, their calling, their faith journey. Pray specifically—for kindness to bloom, for courage to develop, for wisdom to guide their choices. These aren't wishful thoughts; they're powerful petitions to the God who loves your children even more than you do.

When you don't know what to pray, pray Scripture over them. Pray for the fruit of the Spirit to grow in their lives. Pray for protection, purpose, and passion for God. Your prayers are

like seeds planted in heaven's soil, growing into answers you'll harvest in time.

Never doubt that your prayers matter. They're your most powerful mothering tool.

A Prayer for You

Lord, teach me to pray bold, specific prayers for my children. Give me faith to believe You're working even when I can't see it. Help me cover my children consistently in prayer, trusting that my prayers have power to shape their lives and futures. Amen.

Your Challenge

This week, write out one bold, specific prayer for each child. Pray it daily, believing God is working. Watch for small answers and signs of movement. Keep a prayer notebook to track how God responds to your bold requests over time.

Take a Moment

Speak each of your children's names out loud right now, slowly and deliberately. As you say each name, lift that child to God. Your voice speaking their name in prayer is powerful.

Week 13: Teaching Faith One Day at a Time

God's Truth

"You shall teach them diligently to your children, and shall talk of them when you sit in your house, and when you walk by the way, and when you lie down, and when you rise."–Deuteronomy 6:7 (ESV)

Devotional Thought

Teaching faith doesn't require a theology degree or perfect Bible knowledge. It happens in everyday moments—explaining God's provision when bills are tight, pointing out His creation on nature walks, praying together when someone's hurt. Faith is caught more than taught, and your children are watching how you live yours.

Sometimes you worry you're not doing enough. Should you do more devotionals? Memorize more verses? But God's design for faith formation is beautifully simple: weave Him into your ordinary life. Talk about Him naturally, like you'd discuss any family member who's always present.

When your child asks hard questions you can't answer, it's okay to say, "I don't know, but let's find out together." Your willingness to seek God teaches them more than having all the answers. When you mess up and ask forgiveness, you're teaching grace. When you pray about decisions, you're modeling dependence on God.

Faith isn't built in grand gestures but in daily deposits. The bedtime prayers, the mealtime gratitude, the song in the car—these small moments are constructing a foundation that will hold your children through whatever comes.

Trust that your imperfect efforts are enough. God multiplies our offerings, turning our simple faith lessons into deep roots that will sustain your children long after they leave your home.

A Prayer for You

Father, help me teach faith naturally throughout our days. Give me wisdom to recognize teachable moments and courage to share my faith authentically. Use my imperfect efforts to build a strong foundation of faith in my children's hearts. Amen.

Your Challenge

This week, find one everyday moment each day to naturally mention God. Thank Him for the sunset during evening walks. Pray for patience when siblings fight. Celebrate His creativity when examining bugs. Make faith conversations as normal as discussing the weather.

Take a Moment

Picture your children as adults, standing firm in faith during a storm. Your daily faith deposits are building that foundation right now. Trust the process.

Week 14: Building a Faith-Filled Home

God's Truth

"As for me and my house, we will serve the Lord."–
Joshua 24:15b (ESV)

Devotional Thought

A faith-filled home isn't identified by the number of Bible verses on the walls or how perfectly your children behave at church. It's built through countless small decisions to make God central in your family's everyday rhythm. It's choosing to serve the Lord together, imperfectly but consistently.

Your home might not look like that Pinterest-perfect Christian household you imagined. There might be more yelling than you'd like, more rushed prayers than reverent ones, more chaos than peace. But faith is growing in the mess. Every time you choose forgiveness over grudges, you're building faith. Every time you pray through problems instead of panicking, you're laying another brick.

Building a faith-filled home means creating space for God in your family's story. It's talking about His faithfulness at dinner, playing worship music during cleanup, praying for the ambulance you hear passing by. It's showing your children that God isn't just for Sundays—He's woven into the fabric of your daily life.

Your home doesn't need to be perfect to be faith-filled. It just needs to be surrendered. When God is welcomed into your

chaos, He transforms ordinary houses into holy ground where children learn to recognize His voice and follow His ways.

A Prayer for You

Lord, help me build a home where You are honored and welcomed. Show me how to create an atmosphere of faith without perfection. Let my children experience Your presence in our everyday moments, making our home a sanctuary of grace and truth. Amen.

Your Challenge

This week, establish one new faith tradition for your home. It could be blessing your children at bedtime, sharing God-moments at dinner, or playing worship music during breakfast. Start small, be consistent, and watch how this simple addition transforms your home's atmosphere.

Take a Moment

Walk through your home in your mind. Imagine Jesus sitting at your table, playing with your children, present in every room. He's already there—practice recognizing His presence.

Week 15: Seeing Your Family Like God Does

God's Truth

"See what kind of love the Father has given to us, that we should be called children of God; and so we are."–1 John 3:1a (ESV)

Devotional Thought

When you look at your morning chaos—unmade beds, arguing siblings, spilled cereal—you might see failure. But God sees something entirely different. He sees His beloved children (you included) learning and growing, stumbling and getting back up, loved beyond measure despite imperfections.

God doesn't look at your strong-willed child and see defiance; He sees a future leader learning boundaries. He doesn't see your sensitive child as weak; He sees deep compassion being formed. He doesn't see your family's struggles as failures; He sees opportunities for grace to shine.

Sometimes you need to borrow God's eyes to see past the immediate frustration to the eternal work being done. That tantrum isn't just rebellion; it's a child learning emotional regulation with your patient help. Those sibling fights aren't just annoying; they're practice grounds for conflict resolution and forgiveness.

God looks at you not as a failing mother but as His daughter, doing holy work. He sees your exhaustion as evidence of sac-

rifice, your frustration as proof you care, your tears as intercession for your children's hearts.

Today, ask God to help you see your family through His lens of love. Watch how this shift in perspective changes everything—not the circumstances, but how you respond to them.

A Prayer for You

Father, give me Your eyes to see my family. Help me look past behaviors to hearts, past frustration to potential. Show me how deeply You love each member of my family, including me. Transform my vision from critical to compassionate. Amen.

Your Challenge

This week, when frustration rises toward a family member, pause and ask: "How does God see this person right now?" Write down what He might see—their hurt, their growth, their potential. Let His perspective guide your response.

Take a Moment

Close your eyes and picture each family member surrounded by God's golden light of love. See them through that glow. This is how they always look to Him.

Week 16: Grace When You Feel Like You're Failing

God's Truth

"But he gives more grace. Therefore it says, 'God opposes the proud but gives grace to the humble.'"–James 4:6 (ESV)

Devotional Thought

You lost your temper again. Forgot the school project. Served cereal for dinner twice this week. The weight of perceived failures presses heavy, whispering that you're ruining your children, that other moms do this better, that you're just not enough. But here's the truth: God's grace is bigger than your worst day.

Grace isn't just for your children when they make mistakes; it's for you too. God doesn't keep a tally of your mothering failures. He doesn't compare you to other moms. He sees your heart, your efforts, your love—and He pours out grace to cover every gap.

Admitting you're struggling isn't weakness; it's the humble position that invites more grace. When you stop pretending to have it all together, you create space for God's strength to flow. Your children don't need a perfect mother; they need a grace-filled one who shows them what it looks like to receive forgiveness and try again.

Every moment offers a fresh start. The God who renews mercies every morning also renews them every minute. That

failure you're replaying? It's already covered by grace. That mistake you made? It's not the end of your story.

Today, receive the grace you readily give others. Let it wash over your mom-guilt and whisper truth: you're doing better than you think.

A Prayer for You

Lord, I need Your grace today. Forgive my failures and help me forgive myself. Teach me to receive grace as readily as I give it to my children. Replace my guilt with Your peace, knowing Your grace is sufficient for all my shortcomings. Amen.

Your Challenge

This week, when you make a mistake, say out loud: "I receive God's grace for this." Then literally brush your hands together as if wiping it clean. Move forward immediately, refusing to carry guilt that grace has already removed.

Take a Moment

Cup your hands in front of you. Imagine them filling with God's liquid grace, overflowing, more than you can hold. This abundance is available to you every single moment.

Week 17: Trusting God in the Uncertainty

God's Truth

"Trust in the Lord with all your heart, and do not lean on your own understanding. In all your ways acknowledge him, and he will make straight your paths."–Proverbs 3:5-6 (ESV)

Devotional Thought

Will your anxious child find peace? Will your struggling student catch up? Will your teenager make wise choices? Motherhood is an endless exercise in uncertainty, and the not-knowing can keep you awake at night, creating scenarios and searching for control where none exists.

But God isn't surprised by uncertainty. He's already in your child's future, preparing the way, working all things together. Your job isn't to figure everything out or prevent every struggle. It's to trust the One who holds your children's tomorrows in His capable hands.

Trusting God doesn't mean being passive. You still guide, teach, and pray. But trust means releasing the death grip on outcomes you can't control. It means believing God loves your children even more than you do and that His plans for them are good, even when the path looks scary.

When uncertainty threatens to overwhelm you, remember that God is already there. He's in next week's doctor's appointment, next year's decisions, next decade's challenges. Nothing will surprise Him. No situation is beyond His reach.

Today, practice handing your uncertainties to God. Name them, release them, and choose trust over anxiety. Your children need to see you modeling faith in uncertain times.

A Prayer for You

Father, I surrender my need to know and control everything. Help me trust You with my children's futures. When anxiety about uncertainty rises, remind me that You're already working in their tomorrows. Give me peace that passes understanding. Amen.

Your Challenge

Write your biggest uncertainty about each child on a piece of paper. Hold it while praying, then physically place it in a "God box" or drawer. Every time worry returns, remember you've literally given it to God. He's handling it.

Take a Moment

Open your clenched fists and slowly release them, finger by finger. Feel the tension leaving. This is what trusting God feels like—releasing your grip and letting Him hold what you cannot.

Week 18: God's Strength at Your Breaking Point

God's Truth

"My flesh and my heart may fail, but God is the strength of my heart and my portion forever."-
Psalm 73:26 (ESV)

Devotional Thought

You're at the end of yourself. The baby hasn't slept in days, your patience evaporated hours ago, and you're running on fumes and caffeine. You've hit your breaking point, that place where you have absolutely nothing left to give. This is exactly where God does His best work.

Your breaking point isn't your failing point—it's your filling point. When your strength runs out, God's unlimited strength becomes available. He's not waiting for you to get stronger; He's waiting for you to admit you need Him. In your emptiness, He pours out His fullness.

Think about Peter walking on water. He did fine until he relied on his own ability to navigate the storm. The moment he recognized his insufficiency and cried out for help, Jesus immediately reached out. God is reaching for you right now, at your breaking point.

Your children need to see that Mom's strength comes from God. When they watch you rely on Him in your weakness, they learn where to turn in theirs. Your breaking points be-

come teaching points about a God who never breaks, never fails, never runs out of strength.

Right now, at the end of yourself, you're at the beginning of God's supernatural provision.

A Prayer for You

Lord, I'm broken and empty. I have nothing left. Fill me with Your strength. Be strong in my weakness. Help me rely completely on You, knowing that Your power is perfected when I'm at my end. Sustain me with Your unlimited resources. Amen.

Your Challenge

This week, when you hit a breaking point, stop and literally ask God out loud for His strength. Be specific: "God, I need Your patience right now" or "Lord, give me Your energy." Document how He shows up in your weakness.

Take a Moment

Lean back against something solid—a wall, a chair. Feel it holding you up completely. This is God at your breaking point, taking your full weight, holding you when you cannot stand.

Week 19: Let Go of Perfectionism

God's Truth

"For all have sinned and fall short of the glory of God."–Romans 3:23 (ESV)

Devotional Thought

The Pinterest-perfect birthday party. The spotless house. The well-behaved children in matching outfits. Perfectionism whispers that you should achieve all this and more, that good moms don't have messy houses or messy lives. But perfectionism is a prison that keeps you from the freedom found in grace.

God never called you to be perfect; He called you to be faithful. Perfect moms don't exist, but present moms do. Your children don't need a mother who never makes mistakes; they need one who shows them how to handle mistakes with grace.

Perfectionism steals joy from beautiful moments because they don't match your impossible standards. It makes you miss the laughter in the chaos because you're focused on the mess. It exhausts you with its endless demands and leaves you feeling perpetually insufficient.

The truth is, your imperfections are part of God's perfect plan. They keep you dependent on Him, teach your children about grace, and connect you with other struggling moms. Your admitted imperfections give others permission to be real too.

Today, embrace the freedom of being imperfect. Let your children see you laugh at mistakes, adjust expectations, and choose relationship over perfection. Show them that love makes a home, not perfection.

A Prayer for You

Father, free me from perfectionism's impossible standards. Help me embrace the beauty of imperfection and the freedom of grace. Show me that faithfulness matters more than flawlessness. Let me model authentic living for my children, choosing presence over perfection. Amen.

Your Challenge

This week, intentionally leave something imperfect: the bed unmade, the toys scattered, the dinner simple. Notice how the world doesn't end. Practice saying, "Good enough is good enough" and meaning it. Celebrate progress over perfection.

Take a Moment

Hold your hands up and examine them closely. Notice every line, mark, and imperfection. These imperfect hands love perfectly. Your imperfections don't diminish your worth or effectiveness.

Week 20: Discovering Your Inner Strength

God's Truth

"I can do all things through him who strengthens me."–Philippians 4:13 (ESV)

Devotional Thought

You've survived sleepless nights, endless tantrums, and teenage attitudes. You've navigated illnesses, disappointments, and more challenges than you ever imagined. Look at you—you're stronger than you ever knew. This strength isn't self-made; it's God-given, forged in the fires of motherhood.

Sometimes you don't feel strong. You feel fragile, overwhelmed, barely holding on. But strength isn't the absence of struggle; it's persevering through it. Every day you get up and mother again, you're displaying supernatural strength that comes from Christ alone.

Your inner strength shows up in unexpected ways. It's the courage to advocate for your child. The endurance to maintain boundaries. The resilience to start fresh after hard days. The determination to keep loving when you feel unloved. This is kingdom strength, the kind that changes generations.

You're teaching your children about strength not through words but through your example. They're watching you face difficulties with faith, handle pressure with prayer, and keep going when everything in you wants to quit. You're showing them that true strength comes from depending on God.

That reservoir of strength you tap into daily? It's unlimited because it's not yours—it's His, flowing through you.

A Prayer for You

Lord, thank You for the strength You've given me. Help me recognize and trust the inner strength You've developed through motherhood's challenges. When I feel weak, remind me that Your strength is working through me, accomplishing more than I imagine. Amen.

Your Challenge

This week, list five hard things you've survived in motherhood. Beside each one, write how God strengthened you through it. Keep this list as a reminder of the inner strength He's built in you through every challenge.

Take a Moment

Stand and flex your arms like a superhero. You are stronger than you know, not in your own strength but in His. Feel the power God has placed within you.

Week 21: End the Cycle of Mom-Shaming

God's Truth

"Therefore encourage one another and build one another up, just as you are doing."–1 Thessalonians 5:11 (ESV)

Devotional Thought

You've felt the sting of judgment—the look when your child melts down in public, the comment about screen time, the subtle criticism of your parenting choices. Mom-shaming hurts because it attacks you where you're most vulnerable: your deep love for your children and desire to do right by them.

But here's what shame doesn't know: every mother is doing her best with what she has. That mom you're tempted to judge? She's fighting battles you can't see. The one who seems to have it all together? She's questioning herself too. We're all walking this difficult road, making imperfect decisions with imperfect information.

Ending mom-shaming starts with you. When you're tempted to judge another mom's choices, remember you don't know her full story. When you catch yourself comparing, choose compassion instead. When other moms share their struggles, respond with "me too" instead of advice.

The enemy wants mothers divided, judging each other instead of supporting each other. But God calls us to build up, encour-

age, and carry each other's burdens. Your fellow moms aren't your competition; they're your companions in this beautiful, difficult journey.

Today, choose to be a safe place for other mothers. End the shame cycle with grace.

A Prayer for You

Father, forgive me for judging other moms and for accepting shame about my own parenting. Help me encourage instead of criticize, support instead of shame. Make me a safe place for struggling mothers and give me grace for my own journey. Amen.

Your Challenge

This week, genuinely compliment three other moms on something they're doing well. Be specific and sincere. Watch how encouragement lights up their faces. Be part of building a shame-free community where moms support each other.

Take a Moment

Place your hand over your heart and say: "I am the exact mom my children need." Now extend that same grace to every mother you encounter today.

Week 22: Your Online Life Matters

God's Truth

"Let no corrupting talk come out of your mouths, but only such as is good for building up, as fits the occasion, that it may give grace to those who hear."–Ephesians 4:29 (ESV)

Devotional Thought

Your phone holds a window to the world, but sometimes that window becomes a mirror reflecting comparison, negativity, and time-stealing distractions. Your online life affects your real life more than you might realize. What you consume digitally impacts your mood, your mothering, and your family's atmosphere.

Those perfect family photos on Instagram? They're highlight reels, not real life. That argument in the comments section? It's stealing your peace. The endless scrolling when your children want attention? It's creating distance in your closest relationships. Your online habits are shaping your heart and home.

But social media isn't inherently evil. It can connect you with encouragement, resources, and community. The key is intentionality. Follow accounts that inspire rather than intimidate. Share authentically rather than perfectly. Use your platform, however small, to encourage other struggling moms.

Your children are watching how you interact with your phone. They notice when it gets more attention than they do. They see you comparing yourself to others online. They're learning digital habits from your example.

Today, evaluate your online life. Does it build up or tear down? Does it connect or distract? Make changes that honor God and serve your family well.

A Prayer for You

Lord, help me use technology wisely. Guard my heart from comparison and negativity online. Show me how to be salt and light in digital spaces while being fully present with my family. Let my online life reflect Your love and truth. Amen.

Your Challenge

This week, set specific phone-free times: during meals, the first hour after school, or bedtime routines. Notice how your full presence impacts your family. Replace scrolling time with connecting time and see what changes in your home's atmosphere.

Take a Moment

Turn your phone face down or put it in another room for the next ten minutes. Notice any anxiety about disconnecting. This awareness helps you recognize if technology is controlling you rather than serving you.

Week 23: Work, Family, and Finding Balance

God's Truth

"Whatever you do, work heartily, as for the Lord and not for men."—Colossians 3:23 (ESV)

Devotional Thought

Whether you work outside the home, from home, or your work is home, the juggle is real. You're trying to balance professional responsibilities with school pickups, deadline pressures with bedtime stories, career goals with family needs. Some days you feel like you're failing at everything.

Balance isn't about giving equal time to everything—that's impossible. It's about being fully present wherever you are. When you're at work, work heartily for the Lord. When you're with family, be there completely. The guilt that follows you everywhere? It's not from God.

God placed specific gifts and callings in you that extend beyond motherhood. Using them isn't selfish; it's stewardship. Your work, whether paid or volunteer, models diligence for your children. They need to see you contributing your gifts to the world while also prioritizing family.

Some seasons require more work focus; others demand family take precedence. Balance looks different in each season, and that's okay. Stop comparing your balance to others'—their circumstances, support systems, and callings differ from yours.

Trust that God, who called you to both your work and your family, will provide wisdom for managing both. He doesn't call you to anything without equipping you for it.

A Prayer for You

Father, give me wisdom to balance work and family responsibilities. Help me be fully present wherever I am. Remove false guilt and help me trust that You've equipped me for everything You've called me to do. Show me Your priorities each day. Amen.

Your Challenge

This week, identify your top three priorities for this specific season. Make decisions based on these priorities, saying no to good things that don't align. Give yourself permission to do your best in both spheres without perfection in either.

Take a Moment

Hold one hand out representing work and the other representing family. Slowly bring them together, interweaving your fingers. Both can coexist with God's help.

Week 24: Boundaries Without Guilt

God's Truth

"Keep your heart with all vigilance, for from it flow the springs of life." –Proverbs 4:23 (ESV)

Devotional Thought

"Can you volunteer for the bake sale?" "Will you watch my kids?" "Can you take on this project?" Your kind heart wants to say yes to everything, but your exhausted body and overwhelmed schedule scream no. Setting boundaries feels selfish, but it's actually stewardship of the life God's given you.

Boundaries aren't walls that shut people out; they're gates that protect what matters most. When you say no to one thing, you're saying yes to something else—yes to family dinner, yes to rest, yes to being emotionally available for your children. Every no creates space for a better yes.

Jesus himself set boundaries. He withdrew from crowds, said no to certain requests, and prioritized His primary mission. If the Son of God needed boundaries, how much more do you? Boundaries aren't unloving; they're what enable you to love well for the long haul.

That guilt you feel when setting boundaries? It's not from God. He doesn't want you burned out, stretched thin, and resentful. He wants you healthy, whole, and able to serve from abundance rather than depletion.

Your children need to see you model healthy boundaries. They're learning from you how to protect their own hearts, time, and energy.

A Prayer for You

Lord, give me courage to set boundaries without guilt. Help me discern what deserves my yes and what needs my no. Show me that boundaries are loving, both for myself and others. Guard my heart and help me steward my energy wisely. Amen.

Your Challenge

This week, practice saying this: "Let me check my calendar and get back to you." Use this pause before committing to anything. During that pause, pray about whether this request aligns with your current priorities and capacity.

Take a Moment

Draw an imaginary circle around yourself with your finger. This is your boundary line. Inside is what you're responsible for. Outside is what you're not. Feel the freedom of knowing the difference.

Week 25: Quieting the Noise Around You

God's Truth

"Be still, and know that I am God."–Psalm 46:10a (ESV)

Devotional Thought

The TV blares cartoons while notifications ping on your phone. Children argue in the background as the washing machine buzzes. Your mind races with tomorrow's to-do list while today's chaos demands attention. The noise—both external and internal—is deafening. No wonder you can't hear God's still, small voice.

Creating quiet isn't about achieving perfect silence—that's impossible with children. It's about intentionally turning down the volume on things that don't matter so you can tune into what does. It's choosing to switch off the constant input and create space for your soul to breathe.

Sometimes quieting the noise means turning off the TV and letting your family exist without background entertainment. Sometimes it's putting your phone on silent and ignoring non-urgent demands. Sometimes it's saying no to activities that overfill your calendar and overwhelm your family's rhythm.

In the quiet spaces, you'll find what the noise has been drowning out: God's presence, your intuition, your children's hearts. You'll hear the important conversations that get lost in busy

schedules. You'll notice the holy moments hidden in ordinary days.

Your children need quiet too. Their developing minds and spirits need space to process, imagine, and simply be without constant stimulation.

A Prayer for You

Father, help me create quiet spaces in our noisy life. Show me what noise to eliminate and what truly deserves my attention. In the stillness, let me hear Your voice and my children's hearts. Teach me that quiet isn't empty but full of Your presence. Amen.

Your Challenge

This week, institute a daily "quiet time"—not for punishment but for peace. Set a timer for 10-15 minutes where everyone engages in quiet activities. No screens, just books, coloring, or rest. Notice how this reset affects your family's mood.

Take a Moment

Cover your ears for ten seconds, then slowly release. Notice how even temporary quiet changes your awareness. Seek these quiet moments throughout your day.

Week 26: Faith Beyond Sunday

God's Truth

"And these words that I command you today shall be on your heart. You shall teach them diligently to your children, and shall talk of them when you sit in your house, and when you walk by the way, and when you lie down, and when you rise."–
Deuteronomy 6:6-7 (ESV)

Devotional Thought

Sunday church is wonderful, but if faith stays locked in that building, it won't transform your family. Real faith lives in Monday's frustrations, Wednesday's celebrations, and Saturday's chores. It shows up in carpool conversations and bedtime prayers, in discipline moments and dance parties.

Your children are learning what authentic faith looks like by watching you live yours. When they see you pray about lost keys, thank God for parking spaces, and trust Him with big decisions, they learn faith is for real life, not just religious moments.

Faith beyond Sunday doesn't mean preaching constantly or turning every moment into a Bible lesson. It means naturally acknowledging God's presence in your everyday life. It's saying "God helped us today" when problems get solved. It's praying together when someone's scared. It's thanking God for sunsets during evening walks.

Sometimes you worry your faith isn't strong enough to pass on. But God doesn't need your perfect faith; He uses your authentic faith. Your children need to see you questioning and trusting, struggling and believing, falling and getting back up with God's help.

Today, look for ways to weave faith into your regular rhythm. Make God as natural to talk about as weather or homework.

A Prayer for You

Lord, help me live authentic faith that goes beyond Sunday morning. Show me how to naturally incorporate You into our daily conversations and decisions. Let my children see faith that's real, practical, and powerful in everyday life. Make our home a place where You're always acknowledged. Amen.

Your Challenge

This week, share one "God moment" at dinner each night—something you saw God do, provide, or teach that day. Make it natural and brief. Watch how this simple practice helps your family recognize God's daily presence.

Take a Moment

Look at your weekly calendar. Where do you see opportunities to acknowledge God beyond Sunday? In the carpool? During homework? At bedtime? Faith grows in these ordinary moments.

Week 27: When You Feel Spiritually Dry

God's Truth

"As a deer pants for flowing streams, so pants my soul for you, O God."-Psalm 42:1 (ESV)

Devotional Thought

Your Bible sits unopened for weeks. Prayers feel like they bounce off the ceiling. Church feels routine rather than refreshing. You're going through the motions of faith while feeling spiritually empty, wondering if God has withdrawn His presence or if you've somehow failed Him.

Spiritual dryness in motherhood is more common than you think. When you're pouring out constantly—meeting needs, solving problems, giving endlessly—your spiritual well can run dry. You're so busy teaching others about God that you forget to sit with Him yourself.

But here's the truth: God hasn't moved. He's right there in your spiritual desert, waiting patiently. Your feelings don't determine His presence. He's in the mundane tasks, the exhausting nights, the overwhelming days. Sometimes He feels distant because life's noise drowns out His whisper.

Spiritual dryness often precedes spiritual growth. Like ground that must be broken before planting, your dry season is preparing you for deeper roots. God is working even when you can't feel Him, loving you even when you can't sense it.

Start small. A single verse. A two-minute prayer. A worship song while driving. Don't wait for feelings to return before seeking Him. Sometimes obedience comes before emotion, and that's okay.

A Prayer for You

Lord, I feel spiritually empty and distant from You. Revive my dry soul with Your living water. Help me seek You even when I don't feel You. Remind me that You're present in my dryness, working even in my wilderness. Restore my spiritual passion. Amen.

Your Challenge

This week, commit to just five minutes daily with God. Set a timer. Read one psalm or simply sit in His presence. Don't pressure yourself for feelings or profound insights. Just show up consistently and let Him do the rest.

Take a Moment

Cup your empty hands. This represents your spiritual dryness—empty but ready to receive. God fills empty vessels. Your emptiness is actually an invitation for His fullness.

Week 28: Small Steps of Faith

God's Truth

"And Jesus said to them, 'Because of your little faith. For truly, I say to you, if you have faith like a grain of mustard seed, you will say to this mountain, 'Move from here to there,' and it will move, and nothing will be impossible for you.'"–Matthew 17:20 (ESV)

Devotional Thought

You look at other moms leading Bible studies, organizing mission trips, or sharing faith boldly, and you wonder if your small attempts even matter. Your faith steps feel tiny—a whispered prayer over lunch money, a simple "God loves you" at bedtime, a fumbling explanation of heaven. But God specializes in multiplying small offerings.

Remember the boy with five loaves and two fish? His small lunch fed thousands. Your small faith steps have similar potential. That Bible verse you stumble through at breakfast? It might stick in your child's heart forever. That prayer you pray in traffic? It's teaching dependence on God.

Small steps of faith are still steps forward. Reading one verse is better than none. Praying for thirty seconds beats not praying. Attending church tired is more faithful than staying home. God honors every tiny movement toward Him, every mustard seed of faith planted.

Your children don't need to see giant leaps of faith (though those are beautiful too). They need to see consistent, small

steps—daily choices to trust God in ordinary moments. These small steps are building their understanding of what authentic faith looks like.

Today, take one small step. Don't despise it because it seems insignificant. God can move mountains with mustard seeds.

A Prayer for You

Father, help me value small steps of faith instead of waiting for giant leaps. Show me that consistency matters more than size. Give me courage to take the next small step, trusting You to multiply my efforts into kingdom impact. Amen.

Your Challenge

This week, identify one small faith step you can take daily. Maybe it's a prayer before meals, a verse on your mirror, or worship music during chores. Commit to this one small thing consistently and watch how it grows.

Take a Moment

Take one small step forward right now. Feel your weight shift, your body move. Every journey begins with a single step. Your small faith step today leads somewhere beautiful.

Week 29: Trusting God with the Future

God's Truth

"For I know the plans I have for you, declares the Lord, plans for welfare and not for evil, to give you a future and a hope."–Jeremiah 29:11 (ESV)

Devotional Thought

The future stretches before you filled with unknowns. Will your shy child find their voice? Will your rebellious teen find their way back? Will you have wisdom for challenges you can't yet see? The weight of being responsible for shaping futures can paralyze you with fear.

But the future isn't yours to control—it's God's to orchestrate. He's already there, in every tomorrow you're worried about. He sees the whole puzzle while you're holding one piece. His plans for your children were written before they were born, and nothing can derail His purposes.

Trusting God with the future doesn't mean being passive. You still train, guide, and prepare your children. But trust means holding plans loosely, knowing God might have something different—and better—in mind. It means teaching your children to seek God's will above your dreams for them.

Your anxiety about tomorrow is robbing you of today's joy. While you're worrying about teenage years, you're missing the sweetness of elementary days. While you're stressing about college, you're not fully present for high school moments.

God's plans are for hope, not harm. Every challenge your children will face is an opportunity for growth. Every closed door leads to God's better plan. Trust Him with their futures.

A Prayer for You

Lord, I release my children's futures into Your capable hands. Help me trust Your plans over my own. When anxiety about tomorrow rises, remind me You're already there, preparing the way. Give me peace about unknowns and faith in Your good plans. Amen.

Your Challenge

Write a "future letter" to God about each child, naming your hopes and fears for their future. Seal these letters and date them for one year from now. This physical act of giving their futures to God helps release your grip on control.

Take a Moment

Look out a window at the sky. You can't see beyond the horizon, but it continues anyway. God sees the whole view. Trust His perspective over your limited sight.

Week 30: Living Every Day with the Holy Spirit

God's Truth

"But the Helper, the Holy Spirit, whom the Father will send in my name, he will teach you all things and bring to your remembrance all that I have said to you."–John 14:26 (ESV)

Devotional Thought

You have a secret weapon in motherhood that you might be forgetting to access: the Holy Spirit living within you. He's not just for church services or crisis moments. He's available every second of every day, ready to guide, comfort, and empower you through motherhood's challenges.

Need wisdom for a discipline situation? The Holy Spirit offers guidance. Unsure how to answer your child's hard question? He provides words. Out of patience? He supplies supernatural endurance. The Holy Spirit is your ever-present helper in the beautiful chaos of raising children.

But accessing His help requires awareness and invitation. Throughout your day, consciously invite Him into your moments. "Holy Spirit, help me respond with patience." "Show me what this child needs." "Give me Your words." He's waiting for these invitations to partner with you.

Your children need to see you depending on the Holy Spirit. When they watch you pause to pray before responding, they learn about divine help. When they see peace that doesn't

match your circumstances, they witness the Spirit's comfort. You're showing them how to live naturally supernatural lives.

Today, remember you're not mothering alone. The Spirit of God Himself is with you, in you, helping you.

A Prayer for You

Holy Spirit, forgive me for trying to mother in my own strength. Help me remember You're always available. Teach me to invite You into every moment. Speak through me, love through me, and guide me as I guide these children. Amen.

Your Challenge

This week, before responding to any challenging parenting moment, pause and silently invite the Holy Spirit to guide you. Even a two-second pause for His wisdom can completely change your response and the outcome.

Take a Moment

Take a deep breath in, imagining you're breathing in the Holy Spirit's presence. Exhale any stress. He's as close as your breath, as available as air.

Week 31: When Sacrifice Feels Too Much

God's Truth

"Greater love has no one than this, that someone lay down his life for his friends."–John 15:13 (ESV)

Devotional Thought

Another skipped meal because the baby needs feeding. Another postponed dream because kids need stability. Another night of interrupted sleep because someone had a nightmare. The sacrifices pile up until you wonder if there's anything left of you, if the cost of motherhood is too high.

Some days sacrifice feels holy and purposeful. Other days it just feels hard. You watch friends pursue careers while you wipe noses. You see others traveling while you're saving for braces. The sacrifice feels too heavy, too much, too long. Where's the line between healthy sacrifice and losing yourself completely?

But here's what sacrifice knows that you sometimes forget: it's planting seeds for a harvest you can't yet see. Every sacrifice is an investment in eternal souls. Every "no" to yourself that means "yes" to your children's needs is building something that matters more than any personal achievement.

Jesus understands sacrifice. He gave up heaven's glory for earth's mess. He knows what it costs to lay down your life daily. And He promises that sacrifice for love's sake is never wast-

ed, never worthless, never too much when filtered through His grace.

Your sacrifices are seen, valued, and multiplied by the God who sacrificed everything for you.

A Prayer for You

Lord, when sacrifice feels overwhelming, remind me of Your ultimate sacrifice. Help me see the eternal value in my daily laying down of self. Give me strength to sacrifice with joy, knowing You'll restore everything given for love's sake. Amen.

Your Challenge

This week, when you make a sacrifice for your family, consciously offer it to God: "Lord, this is my worship." Transform sacrifice from loss into offering. Notice how this shift changes your perspective from resentment to purpose.

Take a Moment

Hold your arms out in a cross position for ten seconds. Feel the strain. This is sacrifice—uncomfortable but temporary. Lower your arms and feel the relief. Rest always follows sacrifice.

Week 32: Letting Go as Your Kids Grow

God's Truth

"Commit your way to the LORD; trust in him, and he will act." — Psalm 37:5 (ESV)

Devotional Thought

First, you let go of their hand so they could walk. Then you let go of the bike so they could ride. Now you're letting go of bigger things—decisions, friendships, independence. Each release feels like a small death, a tearing of the invisible cord that's connected you since birth.

Letting go doesn't mean loving less; it means loving differently. It's trusting that the roots you've planted run deep enough to hold them. It's believing the wings you've built are strong enough to carry them. It's the ultimate act of faith—releasing what you've protected so fiercely.

But you're not really letting go—you're letting grow. Each release gives them space to become who God created them to be. Your grip, no matter how loving, can't replace their need to develop their own faith, make their own choices, learn their own lessons.

The beautiful truth? You're releasing them to God, not to the world alone. His hands are bigger, stronger, more capable than yours. He loves them more than you do (impossible as that seems). He's got plans for them that require the freedom you're painfully giving.

Today, practice opening your hands a little wider. Trust the training you've given. Trust the God who holds them.

A Prayer for You

Father, letting go is so hard. Help me release my growing children into Your care. Give me wisdom to know when to hold on and when to let go. Remind me that You love them even more than I do. Help me trust Your plans for their lives. Amen.

Your Challenge

This week, identify one area where your child needs more independence. Maybe it's making their own lunch, choosing their clothes, or managing homework. Step back and let them try, even if they don't do it perfectly. Celebrate their growth instead of mourning the change.

Take a Moment

Hold something small and precious in your closed fist. Now slowly open your hand. Notice how the object doesn't fall—it rests safely in your open palm. This is letting go with love.

Week 33: Forgiving Yourself and Moving Forward

God's Truth

"If we confess our sins, he is faithful and just to forgive us our sins and to cleanse us from all unrighteousness."-1 John 1:9 (ESV)

Devotional Thought

That moment you lost your temper keeps replaying. The sharp words you said, the opportunity you missed, the way you failed them—again. You've asked God's forgiveness, but you can't forgive yourself. The weight of mom-guilt is crushing your spirit and stealing your joy.

Here's the truth: refusing to forgive yourself is actually prideful. It suggests your standards are higher than God's, that His forgiveness isn't sufficient. If the Creator of the universe has forgiven you, who are you to withhold forgiveness from yourself?

Your children don't need a perfect mother who never makes mistakes. They need a forgiven mother who shows them what to do with failure. When they see you mess up, apologize, receive forgiveness, and move forward, they learn that mistakes aren't final and grace is real.

Staying stuck in guilt serves no one. It doesn't undo the past or improve the future. It just robs today of its potential. Your children need you present and free, not chained to yesterday's

failures. They need to see that God's mercies really are new every morning.

Today is a fresh start. That mistake you're replaying? It's covered by grace. That failure you're reliving? It's forgiven. Move forward into the freedom Christ died to give you.

A Prayer for You

Lord, I receive Your forgiveness and choose to forgive myself. Help me stop replaying failures and start walking in freedom. Teach me to model grace-filled living for my children. Thank You that Your mercies are new every morning, including this one. Amen.

Your Challenge

Write your recent failures on paper, then literally throw them in the trash or burn them safely. As you do, declare: "I am forgiven and free." When guilt tries to return, remind yourself: "That's in the trash where it belongs."

Take a Moment

Stand up and brush off your shoulders, arms, and legs as if removing dust. This is you brushing off guilt and shame. They don't belong on a forgiven child of God.

Week 34: Celebrate Who You're Becoming

God's Truth

"And I am sure of this, that he who began a good work in you will bring it to completion at the day of Jesus Christ."-Philippians 1:6 (ESV)

Devotional Thought

You might not recognize the woman in the mirror anymore. Motherhood has changed you—your body, your priorities, your capacity for love and worry. Some changes you mourn, but others reveal a strength and beauty you never knew existed. You're becoming someone new, and she's worth celebrating.

The woman you're becoming has learned patience through countless testings. She's developed supernatural endurance through sleepless nights. She's discovered reserves of love she didn't know existed. She's braver, fiercer, softer, and stronger than the woman you were before children.

God is using motherhood to refine you, like gold in fire. Every challenge is removing impurities. Every sacrifice is building character. Every mundane day is shaping you into the image of Christ. You're not the same person you were last year, and that's beautiful.

Stop waiting to celebrate until you've "arrived" at some imaginary finish line. Celebrate the progress—the slightly more patient responses, the growing wisdom, the deepening faith.

Celebrate the woman who gets up every day and loves hard, even when it's hard.

You're a work in progress, and progress is worth celebrating. God isn't finished with you yet, but He's proud of who you're becoming.

A Prayer for You

Father, help me see and celebrate the woman You're forming through motherhood. Thank You for the refining work You're doing in me. Help me embrace who I'm becoming instead of mourning who I was. Continue Your good work in me. Amen.

Your Challenge

This week, list five ways you've grown through motherhood—patience, strength, faith, creativity, anything. Celebrate each growth area. Share this list with someone close to you and let them affirm the beautiful changes they see.

Take a Moment

Look at your reflection in a mirror or window. Say out loud: "I celebrate who I'm becoming." See yourself through God's eyes—a masterpiece in progress.

Week 35: Motherhood Is Your Mission

God's Truth

"And whatever you do, in word or deed, do everything in the name of the Lord Jesus, giving thanks to God the Father through him."-Colossians 3:17 (ESV)

Devotional Thought

Sometimes motherhood feels like a detour from your "real" calling, like you're in a holding pattern until you can pursue your actual mission. But what if motherhood isn't interrupting your mission—what if it IS your mission? What if raising these specific children is exactly what God appointed you to do for such a time as this?

Your mission field is your home. Your disciples are your children. Your ministry happens between diaper changes and homework help. This isn't less-than work; it's kingdom work of the highest order. You're shaping souls, building faith, and launching world-changers from your kitchen table.

Every meal you prepare is communion practice. Every conflict you mediate is peacemaking training. Every bedtime prayer is discipleship. You're not just raising kids; you're raising future parents, spouses, employees, leaders, and disciples. Your motherhood ripples into generations you'll never see.

This mission requires everything you have—your talents, education, experiences, and spiritual gifts. God didn't waste

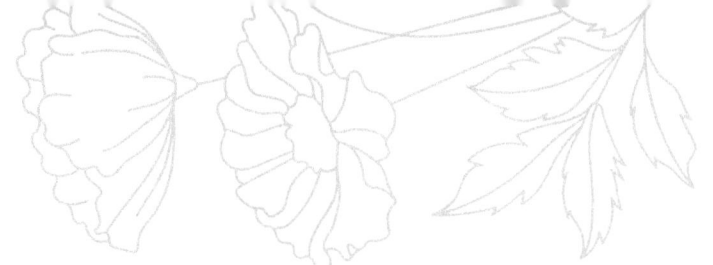

anything He put in you. It's all being used in this holy mission of motherhood, even when it doesn't feel holy at all.

Today, embrace motherhood as the mission it is. You're not waiting for your calling—you're living it.

A Prayer for You

Lord, help me see motherhood as the holy mission You've called me to. Give me purpose in the mundane and vision for the eternal impact of my daily work. Help me embrace this mission with my whole heart, knowing You've equipped me for it. Amen.

Your Challenge

Write a "mission statement" for your motherhood this week. What is God specifically calling you to do with these particular children? Post it where you'll see it daily. Let it remind you that you're on mission, not on hold.

Take a Moment

Place your hand over your heart and commission yourself: "I accept this mission of motherhood. I am called, equipped, and sent by God to raise these children for His glory."

Week 36: Embracing New Beginnings

God's Truth

"Therefore, if anyone is in Christ, he is a new creation. The old has passed away; behold, the new has come."–2 Corinthians 5:17 (ESV)

Devotional Thought

A new school year, a new phase, a new challenge with your children—motherhood is full of new beginnings. Some you welcome with excitement; others you face with dread. But every new beginning is an opportunity for God to do something fresh in your family's story.

Maybe you're starting over after a difficult season. Maybe you're entering unknown territory as your children grow. Maybe you're beginning again after failing yesterday. God specializes in new beginnings. His mercies aren't just new every morning; they're new every moment you need them.

New beginnings require releasing what was to embrace what could be. That means letting go of last year's failures, yesterday's parenting mistakes, or this morning's harsh words. It means believing God can write a new chapter regardless of how the previous one ended.

Your children need to see you embrace new beginnings with faith rather than fear. They need to know that starting over is always possible, that God is the God of second chances and

fresh starts. Your courage in facing new beginnings teaches them resilience.

Today, whatever new beginning you're facing, embrace it with hope. God is doing a new thing. Don't miss it by clinging to what was.

A Prayer for You

Father, help me embrace new beginnings with faith and expectancy. Give me courage to let go of the past and step into the new thing You're doing. Help me model resilience and hope for my children as we face changes together. Amen.

Your Challenge

This week, mark a new beginning in some area of your motherhood. Maybe it's a new routine, a fresh approach to discipline, or renewed commitment to family devotions. Start fresh without guilt about the past. Give yourself the gift of beginning again.

Take a Moment

Open a door in your home and step through it deliberately. This represents stepping into a new beginning. God is on both sides of the threshold, leading you forward.

Week 37: Reflecting on Your Growth

God's Truth

"But grow in the grace and knowledge of our Lord and Savior Jesus Christ. To him be the glory both now and to the day of eternity. Amen."–2 Peter 3:18 (ESV)

Devotional Thought

Pause for a moment and look back. Remember the mom you were when you first held your oldest child? The fears that paralyzed you, the things you didn't know, the strength you hadn't yet developed? Look how far you've come. You've grown in ways you never imagined possible.

Growth in motherhood is often invisible to us because we're too close to see it. But think about it: situations that once sent you into panic now barely raise your pulse. Challenges that felt impossible are now routine. You've developed skills, patience, and wisdom through thousands of small moments.

This growth didn't happen overnight. It came through tears and triumphs, mistakes and victories, ordinary days that built extraordinary strength. Every hard day taught you something. Every challenge grew you. Even your failures contributed to your growth.

God has been faithful through every stage, growing you alongside your children. The same God who helped you through sleepless baby nights is helping you through current

challenges. He's been growing your faith, your character, and your capacity to love.

Take time to acknowledge your growth. Not to become prideful, but to be grateful. Recognizing how far you've come gives you courage for the journey ahead.

A Prayer for You

Lord, thank You for the growth You've produced in me through motherhood. Help me see how far I've come and trust You to continue growing me. Thank You for Your faithfulness through every stage. Give me courage to keep growing and learning. Amen.

Your Challenge

This week, write a letter to your past self—the new mom you once were. Tell her what you've learned, how you've grown, and what you wish you'd known. Celebrate your growth journey and thank God for bringing you this far.

Take a Moment

Stand tall and stretch your arms wide. You're not the same person you were. You've grown taller in faith, wider in love, deeper in wisdom. Feel the expansion.

Week 38: Praying for the Next Chapter

God's Truth

"Call to me and I will answer you, and will tell you great and hidden things that you have not known."–Jeremiah 33:3 (ESV)

Devotional Thought

The next chapter is coming—maybe it's already begun. Your baby is becoming a toddler, your child a teenager, your teenager a young adult. Each transition brings excitement and grief, anticipation and anxiety. You don't know what the next chapter holds, but you know Who holds it.

Prayer is your preparation for unknown chapters. Through prayer, you're writing the story before it unfolds, partnering with God in your family's future. Your prayers today are setting the stage for tomorrow's blessings, protection, and guidance.

Don't wait until the chapter begins to start praying. Pray now for your toddler's teenage years. Pray now for your teenager's future spouse. Pray now for decisions they'll face years from now. Your prayers are going ahead of them, preparing the way.

Praying for the next chapter also prepares your heart. It helps you release control and embrace trust. It shifts your focus from what you might lose to what God might do. It transforms fear into faith, anxiety into anticipation.

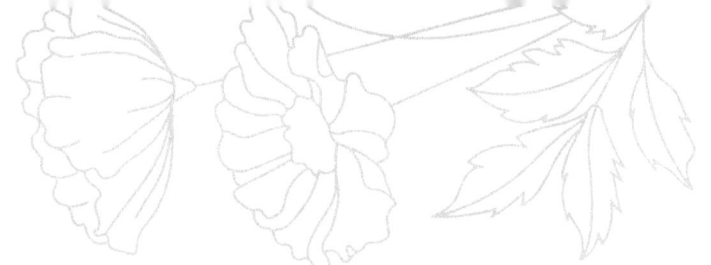

The next chapter might be unknown to you, but it's already written by God. He's prepared good works for your family to walk in. Your prayers align your family's story with His perfect plot.

A Prayer for You

Lord, I lift the next chapter of our family's story to You. Prepare the way for what's coming. Give me wisdom to pray specifically and boldly for each child's future. Help me trust You with chapters I cannot yet read. Write our story for Your glory. Amen.

Your Challenge

This week, dedicate prayer time to each child's next chapter. Be specific—pray for their next school year, life stage, or milestone. Write these prayers down and date them. Watch how God answers as chapters unfold.

Take a Moment

Hold a closed book in your hands. This represents your family's next chapter—written but not yet read. Lift it up to God, trusting the Author with every page.

Week 39: Letting Worry Go

God's Truth

"Therefore do not be anxious about tomorrow, for tomorrow will be anxious for itself. Sufficient for the day is its own trouble."–Matthew 6:34 (ESV)

Devotional Thought

Worry is a mother's unwanted companion. It whispers "what if" scenarios at 2 AM. It magnifies small concerns into crushing fears. It steals today's joy with tomorrow's imagined problems. You worry about their health, their friends, their future, their faith—the list never ends.

But worry accomplishes nothing except robbing you of peace. It doesn't prevent problems or prepare solutions. It just exhausts you with battles that may never happen. Worry is faith in fear rather than faith in God. It's believing the worst instead of trusting the One who works all things for good.

Jesus understands a mother's temptation to worry. That's why He specifically addresses tomorrow's anxieties. He knows you're projecting today's fears into next week, next year, next decade. But He invites you to stay present, to handle today's challenges with today's grace.

Letting worry go doesn't mean you don't care. It means you care enough to entrust your concerns to Someone who can actually do something about them. Every worry is an opportunity to practice trust. Every anxious thought can become a prayer.

Your children are watching how you handle worry. Show them what it looks like to exchange anxiety for peace.

A Prayer for You

Father, I surrender my worries to You. Help me trust You with what I cannot control. When anxiety rises, remind me to pray instead of panic. Give me Your peace that passes understanding. Help me model faith over fear for my children. Amen.

Your Challenge

This week, create a "worry window"—set aside 10 minutes daily to write down worries, pray over them, then close the notebook. When worries arise outside this window, tell them to wait for their designated time. This contains worry instead of letting it consume your day.

Take a Moment

Take a deep breath and as you exhale, blow out your worries like candle flames. Watch them dissipate into the air. They have no power when released to God.

Week 40: Walking in God's Purpose

God's Truth

"For we are his workmanship, created in Christ Jesus for good works, which God prepared beforehand, that we should walk in them."-
Ephesians 2:10 (ESV)

Devotional Thought

You might think God's purpose for your life is on hold while you're raising children, but motherhood isn't a detour from your purpose—it's central to it. Every diaper changed, every meal prepared, every homework session supervised is you walking in the good works God prepared specifically for you.

Your purpose isn't just about what you do but who you're becoming and who you're raising. God orchestrated your life to intersect with these specific children at this exact time. Your unique personality, gifts, and even your struggles equip you for the purpose of mothering these particular souls.

Walking in God's purpose doesn't always feel purposeful. Some days it feels mundane, exhausting, invisible. But purpose isn't always glamorous. Sometimes it looks like faithfulness in small things, obedience in the ordinary, perseverance when no one's watching.

Your purpose extends beyond your children but includes them fully. The gifts God placed in you aren't diminished by motherhood; they're refined by it. Your purpose is multi-faceted—

raising kingdom kids while being the woman God created you to be.

Today, walk confidently in your purpose. Every mundane task has eternal significance when done for God's glory. You're exactly where you're supposed to be.

A Prayer for You

Lord, help me recognize and embrace Your purpose for my life in this season. Show me how motherhood fits into Your bigger picture for me. Give me confidence that I'm walking in the works You prepared beforehand, even in ordinary moments. Amen.

Your Challenge

This week, identify three ways your unique gifts and personality specifically equip you to mother your children. Write them down and thank God for purposefully designing you for this calling. See yourself as chosen, not accidental, for this role.

Take a Moment

Stand and take three purposeful steps forward. Each step represents walking in God's purpose. You're not wandering; you're walking in prepared paths.

Week 41: Every Mom Win Matters

God's Truth

"His master said to him, 'Well done, good and faithful servant. You have been faithful over a little; I will set you over much.'"-Matthew 25:21 (ESV)

Devotional Thought

Today's wins might seem small. Everyone ate breakfast. You read that story with enthusiasm despite exhaustion. You bit your tongue instead of yelling. These victories don't make headlines or social media posts, but heaven celebrates every single one.

We often dismiss our mom wins because they seem ordinary compared to others' highlights. But God doesn't measure success like the world does. He celebrates faithfulness in little things. That patience you showed during the twentieth "Mom, watch this!"? That matters. The hundredth lunch you packed with love? That counts.

Every mom win is building something bigger than you can see. Consistent small victories create children who feel loved, secure, and valued. Your daily wins are writing their childhood narrative, one ordinary moment at a time. These seemingly insignificant triumphs are actually eternal investments.

Stop waiting for big victories to celebrate. Your child said "please" without prompting—win! Everyone survived grocery shopping—victory! You chose connection over perfection—

triumph! These small wins accumulate into transformed lives, both yours and theirs.

God sees every win, every effort, every time you choose love when you're depleted. He's keeping score differently than you are, and by His count, you're winning more than you know.

A Prayer for You

Father, help me recognize and celebrate small victories instead of dismissing them. Thank You for seeing every faithful act, every patient response, every loving gesture. Remind me that small wins matter greatly in Your kingdom. Help me encourage other moms in their wins too. Amen.

Your Challenge

This week, celebrate three mom wins each day, no matter how small. Share one win daily with a friend or family member. Build a culture of celebrating ordinary victories. Notice how acknowledging wins changes your perspective on your mothering.

Take a Moment

Give yourself a literal pat on the back right now. You're doing better than you think. Every small win is worth celebrating.

Week 42: Raising Faith-Filled Kids

God's Truth

"Train up a child in the way he should go; even when he is old he will not depart from it."-Proverbs 22:6 (ESV)

Devotional Thought

Raising faith-filled kids feels overwhelming when you see the world they're growing up in. The culture pulls one way while you're desperately pulling another. You wonder if family devotions and bedtime prayers are enough to combat the messages bombarding them daily.

But faith isn't transferred through perfect programs or flawless theology. It's caught through authentic living. Your children are learning faith by watching you navigate struggles with prayer, celebrate blessings with gratitude, and trust God when life doesn't make sense.

Faith-filled kids aren't created through force but through environment. When faith is the natural atmosphere of your home—woven into conversations, decisions, and daily rhythms—it becomes as natural to them as breathing. They absorb what they're immersed in.

Don't panic when they question or doubt; that's actually faith developing. Wrestling with God is still engaging with Him. Your job isn't to have all the answers but to point them to the

One who does. Show them that faith is strong enough to handle hard questions.

The seeds you're planting through simple prayers, Bible stories, and faith conversations are taking root deeper than you can see. Trust the process. God is faithful to complete what you're beginning.

A Prayer for You

Lord, give me wisdom to raise children who love and follow You. Help me model authentic faith that draws them to You. Use my imperfect efforts to plant deep roots of faith that will sustain them through every season of life. Amen.

Your Challenge

This week, share one personal faith story with your children—a time God answered prayer, provided unexpectedly, or gave you peace. Let them see faith isn't just Bible stories but your story too. Make faith personal and real through your testimony.

Take a Moment

Picture your children as adults, standing firm in faith. Every prayer, every Bible story, every faith conversation is building toward that future. Trust the foundation you're laying.

Week 43: Overcoming Fear for Your Family

God's Truth

"For God gave us a spirit not of fear but of power and love and self-control."–2 Timothy 1:7 (ESV)

Devotional Thought

Fear for your family can be paralyzing. Fear of illness, accidents, bad influences, wrong choices—the list of potential dangers feels endless. News headlines fuel your anxiety. Other people's tragedies become your imagined possibilities. Fear whispers that you can't protect them from everything, and it's right—you can't.

But you were never meant to be their ultimate protector. That's God's job. Your job is to trust the One who never sleeps, who sees dangers you can't, who loves them infinitely more than you do. Fear isn't from God; it's a tool the enemy uses to steal your peace and joy.

Overcoming fear doesn't mean ignoring real dangers. It means taking reasonable precautions while refusing to be controlled by "what ifs." It means praying instead of panicking, trusting instead of controlling, believing God's promises instead of fear's lies.

Your children absorb your fears. When they see you consumed with anxiety about their safety, they learn the world is scary and God isn't sufficient. But when they see you face fears with

faith, they learn courage. They discover that perfect love—God's love—really does cast out fear.

Today, name your fears and hand them to God. He's big enough to handle them and trustworthy enough to protect what you treasure most.

A Prayer for You

Father, I confess my fears for my family. Replace my spirit of fear with Your power, love, and self-control. Help me trust You as their ultimate protector. Give me wisdom to prepare without panicking, to protect without controlling. Let faith be stronger than fear. Amen.

Your Challenge

This week, when fear for your family rises, immediately turn it into specific prayer. Transform "What if something bad happens?" into "God, I trust You to protect them." Keep a record of how God protects your family, building evidence of His faithfulness.

Take a Moment

Hold your hands out with palms up, then flip them over, releasing your fears to God. You cannot carry what you've released to Him.

Week 44: Finding Peace in Hard Days

God's Truth

"Peace I leave with you; my peace I give to you. Not as the world gives do I give to you. Let not your hearts be troubled, neither let them be afraid."- *John 14:27 (ESV)*

Devotional Thought

Today might be one of those hard days. The kind where everything goes wrong, everyone needs something, and you're running on empty. Peace feels impossible when chaos reigns and problems multiply. But Jesus offers a different kind of peace—one that exists despite circumstances, not because of them.

His peace isn't the absence of trouble; it's His presence in trouble. It's the inexplicable calm in your spirit even when your world is spinning. This peace doesn't make sense to outsiders because it's not based on situations being perfect but on God being present.

Finding peace on hard days requires intentional choosing. Choose to breathe deeply and remember God is in control. Choose to lower your expectations and raise your prayers. Choose to believe this hard day is held by the same God who holds your good days.

Your children need to see you access peace when life is difficult. They need to know peace is possible even in problems.

When they watch you find calm in chaos through God's presence, they learn where to anchor their own hearts during storms.

This hard day will end. But the peace God gives you in it can sustain you through whatever comes next.

A Prayer for You

Lord, I need Your peace that passes understanding. When my day is hard and my heart is troubled, be my peace. Help me access the calm You offer despite my circumstances. Let Your peace guard my heart and mind today. Amen.

Your Challenge

This week, create a "peace practice" for hard moments: stop, take five deep breaths while repeating "Jesus, You are my peace." Use this practice multiple times daily. Notice how pausing to receive His peace changes your capacity to handle difficulties.

Take a Moment

Place your hand on your heart. Feel its steady rhythm. Even in chaos, it keeps beating steadily. This is God's peace—steady, constant, reliable despite external storms.

Week 45: Encouraging Yourself in Faith

God's Truth

"And David was greatly distressed, for the people spoke of stoning him... But David strengthened himself in the Lord his God."–1 Samuel 30:6 (ESV)

Devotional Thought

Sometimes no one else understands the weight you're carrying. Friends try to help but don't quite get it. Your spouse supports you but can't fully comprehend the mental load of motherhood. In these moments, like David, you must learn to encourage yourself in the Lord.

Encouraging yourself isn't positive self-talk or denial of difficulties. It's actively reminding yourself of God's truth when feelings scream lies. It's preaching the gospel to your own heart when discouragement threatens to overwhelm. It's choosing to remember God's faithfulness when today feels impossible.

You know how to encourage others—you do it for your children constantly. Now turn that gift inward. Speak truth to yourself: God chose you for these children. He equips you daily. His mercies are new every morning. You're doing better than you think. He's proud of your efforts.

Sometimes you have to be your own cheerleader because you're the only one who knows the battles you're fighting. But

you're never really alone in the encouragement. The Holy Spirit is called the Encourager, and He lives within you.

Today, encourage yourself with God's truth. Don't wait for someone else to notice your struggles or affirm your efforts. Strengthen yourself in the Lord.

A Prayer for You

Lord, when discouragement overwhelms me, teach me to encourage myself in You. Help me remember Your truths, Your faithfulness, Your promises. Give me strength to preach hope to my own heart. Be my encouragement when no one else understands. Amen.

Your Challenge

This week, write yourself an encouragement note each morning. Include a Bible verse and specific affirmation about your mothering. Read it when discouragement strikes. Be your own encourager, speaking God's truth over yourself.

Take a Moment

Look yourself in the eyes in a mirror and speak this truth: "I am loved, equipped, and chosen by God for this calling." Believe it.

Week 46: Rediscovering Your Passion

God's Truth

"Therefore I remind you to fan into flame the gift of God, which is in you."–2 Timothy 1:6a (ESV)

Devotional Thought

Remember those things that once made your heart race with excitement? The dreams, hobbies, and interests that defined you before "Mom" became your primary identity? They might feel buried under laundry piles and school schedules, but those passions are still there, embers waiting to be rekindled.

God gave you passions for a purpose. They're not selfish pursuits to abandon for motherhood; they're part of how He designed you. Your children need to see you as a whole person with interests, dreams, and gifts. It teaches them that motherhood doesn't mean losing yourself.

Rediscovering passion might start small. Five minutes sketching while kids nap. A podcast about your interest during commutes. An online class after bedtime. You don't need huge blocks of time to keep passions alive; you just need intention.

Your passions might look different in this season. Maybe you can't travel the world, but you can plan family adventures. Maybe you can't perform on stage, but you can sing lullabies. Your passions can evolve to include your children while still feeding your soul.

Fan those embers back to flame. Your family needs a mom who's alive with purpose and passion, not just surviving each day.

A Prayer for You

Lord, help me rediscover the passions You placed within me. Show me how to nurture my gifts while nurturing my children. Give me wisdom to pursue passions in ways that bless my family. Remind me that You created me with purpose beyond motherhood alone. Amen.

Your Challenge

This week, spend thirty minutes total on something you're passionate about—even if it's broken into six five-minute segments. Notice how feeding your passion affects your energy and joy. Make this a weekly non-negotiable, gradually increasing as possible.

Take a Moment

Close your eyes and remember the last time you felt truly excited about something. Hold that feeling. That spark is still in you, waiting to be fanned into flame.

Week 47: God Fills the Gaps

God's Truth

"And my God will supply every need of yours according to his riches in glory in Christ Jesus."-Philippians 4:19 (ESV)

Devotional Thought

You're painfully aware of your gaps—patience that runs out, wisdom you lack, energy that depletes, resources that fall short. Every day reveals new ways you're not enough for this calling. The gaps between what your children need and what you can give feel impossibly wide.

But here's the beautiful truth: God specializes in filling gaps. Where your patience ends, His continues. Where your wisdom fails, His prevails. Where your strength runs out, His kicks in. He doesn't expect you to be sufficient; He promises to be sufficient for you.

Those gaps you're so worried about? They're not failures; they're opportunities for God to show up. Your children need to see that Mom doesn't have everything, but she knows Who does. They need to witness God providing when you can't, answering when you don't know, strengthening when you're weak.

Stop trying to eliminate all gaps through your own effort. Some gaps are meant to remain so God's power can be displayed. Your insufficiency isn't a disqualification; it's an invitation for His all-sufficiency.

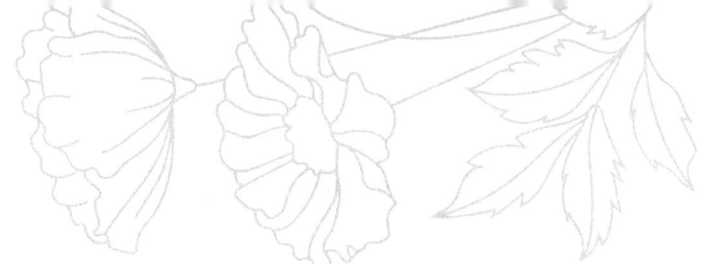

Today, instead of stressing about gaps, invite God to fill them. Watch Him supply exactly what your family needs from His unlimited resources.

A Prayer for You

Father, I bring You my gaps—all the ways I'm not enough. Thank You for promising to supply every need. Fill the spaces between what I can give and what my children need. Let them see Your provision through my insufficiency. Amen.

Your Challenge

This week, identify your three biggest "gap" areas in mothering. Instead of trying harder to fill them yourself, specifically ask God to fill them. Document how He provides what you lack. Watch Him work in your weakness.

Take a Moment

Cup your hands, leaving space between them. This gap represents your insufficiency. Now bring them together. This is God filling every gap with His sufficiency.

Week 48: Speak Blessings Over Your Family

God's Truth

"Death and life are in the power of the tongue, and those who love it will eat its fruits."–Proverbs 18:21 (ESV)

Devotional Thought

Your words carry more power than you realize. They can build up or tear down, inspire or discourage, bless or curse. In the rush of daily life, it's easy to let correction and criticism dominate while blessings remain unspoken. But your family needs to hear life-giving words from the one whose opinion matters most.

Speaking blessings isn't about empty flattery or ignoring problems. It's about calling out the gold in your family members, speaking to their potential, declaring God's truth over their lives. It's saying "You're going to do great things" to your struggling student. It's telling your difficult child "God has amazing plans for your strong will."

Your children will face enough criticism from the world. Home should be where they're filled with words of life, where their tanks are filled with encouragement. They need to hear not just "I love you" but "I see God working in you" and "I'm proud of who you're becoming."

Blessings spoken over your family become anchors in their souls. Years from now, they'll remember your words of life

during moments of doubt. Your blessings today become their strength tomorrow.

Make blessing your family a daily practice. Watch how your words shape their becoming.

A Prayer for You

Lord, help me speak life and blessings over my family. Give me eyes to see their potential and words to call it forth. Let my tongue be an instrument of encouragement and hope. Help me build them up with my words daily. Amen.

Your Challenge

This week, speak one specific blessing over each family member daily. Look them in the eyes and declare something true and encouraging about who they are or who they're becoming. Watch how these blessings change both them and your family's atmosphere.

Take a Moment

Place your fingers on your lips. These lips have power to bless or hurt. Choose now to use them for life, speaking blessings that echo in eternity.

Week 49: God's Grace in the Everyday

God's Truth

"But he said to me, 'My grace is sufficient for you, for my power is made perfect in weakness.'"–2 Corinthians 12:9a (ESV)

Devotional Thought

Grace isn't just for salvation or major failures. It's for Tuesday afternoon meltdowns, Thursday morning rushing, and Saturday sibling fights. God's grace is as available for everyday moments as it is for life-changing ones. It's new every morning and renewed every moment you need it.

You might think of grace as God's response to sin, but it's also His provision for inadequacy. Grace is what enables you to respond patiently the tenth time. Grace is finding energy you don't have. Grace is wisdom appearing when you're clueless. It's God's supernatural enabling for natural life.

In the everyday mundane, grace shows up as unexpected patience, surprising joy, and strength you can't explain. It's laughing when you could cry, trying again when you want to quit, choosing love when you feel empty. These grace moments are miracles disguised as ordinary life.

Your children need to see grace in action—not just talked about but lived out. When they watch you extend grace to them and yourself, they learn what God's grace looks like. Your everyday grace teaches them about His extraordinary grace.

Today, watch for grace. It's there in your everyday moments, sufficient for whatever you face.

A Prayer for You

Father, thank You for grace that covers my everyday needs, not just my enormous failures. Help me recognize and receive Your grace in ordinary moments. Let me be a channel of grace to my family, showing them Your sufficiency in daily life. Amen.

Your Challenge

This week, identify one grace moment each day—a time when God's strength showed up in your weakness. Share these grace sightings with your family at dinner. Help everyone recognize God's everyday grace in ordinary moments.

Take a Moment

Hold out your empty hands. Now imagine them filling with God's grace—abundant, overflowing, more than enough for today. This grace is yours for the taking.

Week 50: Quiet Time, Restored Soul

God's Truth

"He makes me lie down in green pastures. He leads me beside still waters. He restores my soul."–Psalm 23:2-3a (ESV)

Devotional Thought

Your soul feels frayed from constant giving, deciding, and managing. You pour out continuously but rarely refill. Quiet time feels like a luxury you can't afford when everyone needs something now. But a depleted soul can't nurture other souls. You need restoration to continue giving.

God isn't suggesting rest; He's commanding it. "He makes me lie down"—sometimes God has to force rest because you won't choose it. But this isn't punishment; it's provision. He knows you need still waters for your soul to be restored. Without quiet refilling, you'll run dry.

Quiet time doesn't require a weekend retreat or hours of solitude. It might be five minutes before everyone wakes, a prayer walk around the block, or sitting in your car for a moment before entering the house. Small sips of stillness can restore a weary soul.

Your children need to see you prioritize soul care. When they watch you protect quiet time with God, they learn that spiritual health matters. They understand that even Mom needs restoration, that running on empty serves no one.

Today, find a pocket of quiet. Let God restore what motherhood has depleted. Your soul needs those still waters.

A Prayer for You

Lord, my soul is weary and frayed. Lead me to still waters where You restore souls. Help me prioritize quiet time with You without guilt. Show me how to find moments of restoration in my busy life. Refill what constant giving has emptied. Amen.

Your Challenge

This week, protect ten minutes of daily quiet time—before kids wake, during naps, or after bedtime. Use this time just to be still with God. No agenda, no requests, just restoration. Notice how this small investment pays huge dividends.

Take a Moment

Sit still for sixty seconds. No phone, no movement, just stillness. Feel your soul settling, like stirred water becoming clear. This is what quiet time does—it clarifies and restores.

Week 51: Purpose in Every Season

God's Truth

"For everything there is a season, and a time for every matter under heaven."-Ecclesiastes 3:1 (ESV)

Devotional Thought

The baby season with its sleepless nights. The toddler season with its constant motion. The school-age season with its endless activities. The teen season with its emotional complexity. Every season of motherhood brings unique challenges and hidden purposes. God wastes no season in your life.

You might wish away certain seasons, eager for the next phase when things will be "easier." But every season has specific purposes God wants to accomplish—in your children and in you. The patience learned in toddler tantrums prepares you for teenage attitudes. The prayer habits developed through elementary struggles equip you for bigger battles ahead.

This current season, whatever it holds, has purpose. Maybe it's teaching you dependence on God. Maybe it's developing character in your children. Maybe it's preparing all of you for what's coming next. Don't miss today's purpose wishing for tomorrow's season.

Some seasons feel longer than others. Some feel harder. But each one is perfectly timed by a God who knows exactly what your family needs. He's using this season to shape, refine, and prepare you all for His plans.

Embrace this season's purpose, even if you don't fully understand it. Trust that God is working in the waiting, growing in the difficulty, preparing in the present.

A Prayer for You

Lord, help me find and embrace Your purpose in this current season. When I want to rush through or wish it away, remind me You're working right now. Give me eyes to see what You're doing and patience to let this season complete its work. Amen.

Your Challenge

This week, write down three purposes you see in your current season—lessons being learned, character being built, or preparation happening. Thank God for this season's specific work. Share with your children what God is teaching you in this season.

Take a Moment

Look at a tree outside your window or imagine one. It's beautiful in every season—budding, blooming, changing, resting. You're beautiful in every season too, each one serving God's purpose.

Week 52: Boldly Step Into God's Plans

God's Truth

"Have I not commanded you? Be strong and courageous. Do not be frightened, and do not be dismayed, for the Lord your God is with you wherever you go."–Joshua 1:9 (ESV)

Devotional Thought

Here you stand at the threshold of another year, carrying all you've learned, all you've overcome, all you've become. God has plans for your family that require bold faith, courageous steps, and trust beyond what feels comfortable. This is your moment to step forward boldly into all He has prepared.

Looking back, you can see His faithfulness through every challenge. Looking forward, you can trust that same faithfulness continues. The God who carried you through this year is already in your next year, preparing the way, working all things for good.

Bold steps don't mean you're not afraid; they mean you're more confident in God than in your fears. It's choosing to follow His leading even when the path isn't clear. It's saying yes to His plans even when they stretch you beyond comfort. It's trusting His presence more than your own understanding.

Your children need to see you step boldly into God's plans. They need to witness faith that moves forward despite uncertainty, that trusts God's promises over visible circumstances.

Your bold faith gives them permission to live courageously too.

This year, don't hold back. Step boldly into everything God has planned. He's with you wherever He leads.

A Prayer for You

Lord, give me courage to step boldly into Your plans for my family. Increase my faith to match Your calling. Help me lead my children in courageous faith. Thank You for Your presence that goes with us wherever You lead. Here we go, Lord—we're ready. Amen.

Your Challenge

This week, identify one bold step God is asking you to take with your family. Write it down, pray over it, then take the first small action toward it. Mark this moment as when you chose faith over fear, boldness over comfort.

Take a Moment

Stand at a doorway in your home. This represents the threshold of God's plans. Take a deep breath and step through boldly. He's with you wherever you go.

Discover More Books

Start each day with purpose, peace, and a deeper connection to God. Whether you're nurturing your own faith, guiding your children, or growing together as a family—this devotional series meets you right where life happens.

Collect the Whole Series

| Devotional for Dads | Devotional for Moms | Devotional for Kids |

Available at major online bookstores

Each book is a spiritual companion—designed to inspire, uplift, and transform. Together, they form a complete journey of faith for the whole family.

Don't wait—bring home the full set and let every day draw you closer to God, to each other, and to the life you were created for.